Sands from the River of Timelessness

Sands from the River of Timelessness

POEMS INSPIRED BY THE TAO TE CHING AND THE INTEGRAL WAY

N. MICHAEL MURBURG, JR.

PALMETTO

PUBLISHING

Charleston, SC

www.PalmettoPublishing.com

Hardcover ISBN: 979-8-8229-5507-3
Paperback ISBN: 979-8-8229-5508-0
eBook ISBN: 979-8-8229-5509-7

DEDICATION

This book of Tao poems is first dedicated to my friend and fellow painter and poet Elliot Greenbaum who when I explained what I wanted to do and showed him a few of the early works said "I think you may be on to something. Go run with it." And so, I did. Thank you, El. Even though you were not familiar with the subject or form, without your support and encouragement, this book may not have ever come into being. Sorry for the wait. I would also like to dedicate this book of poems to my daughter who gave me three wonderful grandchildren between the time I began writing this book and the time it was finished. Finally, I would like to dedicate this book to Leslie Meekins, whose sharp eyes and keen sense of the Tao allowed me to correct my mistakes and ready these poems for publication.

THE SANDS OF THE "RIVER OF TIMELESSNESS"

UNIVERSAL SUBTLE ESSENCE
UNFAILING, VAST AND PROFOUND.
PRIMAL FEMALE,
THE GREAT TAI CHI,
MYSTERIOUS ORIGIN,
SEEN AND UNSEEN
MYSTICAL INTERCOURSE
OF YIN AND YANG,
YOU BRING FORTH
THE SANDS FROM YOUR RIVER OF
TIMELESSNESS
FOR OUR CREATION AND USE.
INDISCRIMINATE LOVE AND COMPASSION,
ETERNAL MOTHER,
IN ALL SOFTNESS,
YOU ARE SACRED.

TABLE OF CONTENTS

1.

TAO,
FORMLESS,
NAMELESS,
MYSTERIOUS
TIMELESSNESS.

UNDERSTANDING TAO
IN THE HEART OF ETERNAL DARKNESS,
THE WAY DOES BEGIN.

2.

EXTREMES
DEFINE NOTHING.
TO BE
IS
TO NOT TO BE.

WISE IS THE MASTER
WHO IN GIVING ALL
WITHOUT EXPECTATION
OR DISCRIMINATION
ALWAYS HAS
WHATEVER SHE NEEDS.

LIKE THE INEXHAUSTIBLE TAO,
ALWAYS MOVING
AND FLOWING,

SILENT IS
HER WORK.

THE MASTER RESTS
YET NOTHING
REMAINS
UNFINISHED.

3.

THE OVER ESTEEMED
WEAKEN THE ESTEEMER

DESIRE MAKES MANY THIEVES.
OWNING LITTLE,
THE MASTER
INTENTIONALLY DOES NOTHING.

AND THROUGH WU WEI
BY DOING NOTHING
HE ALLOWS
HARMONY
EVERYWHERE
TO THRIVE.

4.

TAO,
WELLSPRING OF THE INFINITE

HIDDEN
MOST ANCIENT MOTHER OF ALL

THE BOSOM FROM WHICH
ALL GODS WERE BORN
AND FROM WHICH
ALL IN HER CREATION FLOW.

5.

UNIVERSAL TAO,
VACUOUS,
ETERNAL,
UNCENTERED
CENTER OF ALL
STRIVES
FOR
CONSTANT
BALANCE.

6.

TAO
THE ALL
MIGHTY
MOTHER
OF INFINITE BEINGS
BIRTHER
OF INNUMERABLE WORLDS
SHE CONTINUALLY SERVES THE NEEDS
OF ALL
HER CHILDREN.

7.

IMMORTAL TAO
INFINITE,
TIMELESS PRESENCE
AT HER
CENTER
SHE
IS
ONE WITH ALL.

8.

THE TAO

A

O

LIKE WATER,

OMNIPRESENT

EFFORTLESSLY FLOWING

FROM HIGH

TO LOW.

SIMPLE,

PURE,

GROUNDED AND ELEMENTAL,

COMMANDING NOT,

SHE IS RESPECTED.

AND JOYFULLY,

LIKE THE MASTER

SHE SERVES ALL.

9.

THE FULL VESSEL
EASILY SPILLS.

THE KNIFE
OVER-SHARPENED
QUICKLY DULLS.

THE TRUE HEART
PURSUES NEITHER WEALTH NOR APPROVAL,
AS IT SEEKS TO DO ITS WORK,
AND THEN
LETS GO

SO THAT THE TAO MAY COME AND COMPLETE
IT.

10.

BE STILL MY CHILD.
TO UNDERSTAND
BE SUPPLE.
TO TRULY GIVE BIRTH,
ONE MUST ALSO NOURISH.

WILL YOU NOT LOOK TO THE STILL ONENESS
WITHIN
AND TO YOUR INTERNAL LIGHT TO LOVE AND
LEAD ALL
BY ITS SUPREME VIRTUE
TO ACT
WITHOUT EXPECTATION,

TO LEAD
YET NOT CONTROL,

TO HAVE
BUT NOT POSSESS,

TO UNDERSTAND,
YET NOT KNOW ALL,

TO DO
BY LETTING ALL THINGS FLOW.

11.

BEING AND NONBEING,
AT THE CENTER
OF EVERY USEFUL THING
IS EMPTINESS.

ONE IS AT ONE'S MOST USEFUL
WHEN ONE'S CENTER HAS YET TO BE FILLED.

12.

THE SENSES NUMB.
DESIRE POISONS.
THOUGHT ENFEEBLES

WITH THE WORLD OBSERVED
AND ALLOWED
TO COME AND GO,

UNATTACHED WITHIN,
AND COMPASSIONATELY IN LOVE WITH ALL,
DOES THE MASTER
THERE ABIDE.

13.

SUCCESS AND FAILURE
HOPE AND FEAR
EGO AND THE OPINIONS OF OTHERS:
TWO FACES OF THE SAME WORTHLESS COIN.
BALANCE
AND FAITH IN THE WAY THINGS ARE
COMES TO HIM
WHO REMAINS INTERNALLY GROUNDED
AND ROOTED DEEPLY
IN THE TAO.

14.

TAO IS ALL YET NOTHING
ETERNALLY BEYOND BUT ALWAYS PRESENT.

THE MASTER UNDERSTANDS.
THE MOTHER OF THE STREAM
IS NOT THE MOUNTAIN
BUT THE SEA.

BOTH HAVE THE SAME SOURCE

15.

PATIENTLY, LIKE A BLOCK OF WOOD
THE MASTER SHAPES HIMSELF.

LIKE WELL WARMED TEA
WHOSE WATER AND LEAVES HAVE SETTLED,
INVITING
REFINED
WARMING,
WITH COMPLETE PRESENCE AND CARE,

THUS, DOES THE MASTER ACT.

16.

SERENITY
IS THE MOTHER OF PEACE.
SERENITY COMES FROM FLOW
FLOW COMES FROM SOURCE.

SOURCE IS ALL
ALL IS SOURCE.

EVERYTHING IN BETWEEN IS A
WONDERMENT.

IN UNDERSTANDING THAT ALL THINGS
RETURN TO SOURCE,
ETERNAL PEACE LIES.

17.

GREAT IS THE LEADER
WHO LEADS BY EXAMPLE.

TRUSTING ALL TO THEIR TASKS,
THE GREAT MASTER GOES UNNOTICED.

18.

WITHOUT THE GREAT TAO
SADLY, PEACE WILL BE FORGOTTEN
AND INTO CHAOS ALL WILL FALL.

19.

HAPPINES LIES NOT
IN HOLINESS OR WISDOM
MORALITY OR JUSTICE, INDUSTRY OR GAIN,
BUT IN STAYING TRUE TO ONE'S ORIGINAL
SELF
AND REMAINING BALANCED
AND WELL CENTERED.

20.

NO MAN
CAN CONTROL
EITHER THE WINDS OR TIDES.

ABOVE THE FLOW
THE FEATHER RIDES,
FREE AND
WITHOUT DIRECTION IT FLIES,
YET ALWAYS SOFT IS ITS LANDING.

21.

TAO
INFINITE,
AGELESS,
ELUSIVE
AND
EVADING,

BEYOND ALL
SHE UNVEILS HER RADIANCE.
HER DEEP VIRTUE
BEARS
AND
CHERISHES ALL.

RADIANT MOTHER,
TIMELESS BEAUTY,
WE KNOW YOUR OCEANS
WITHIN A SINGLE TEAR.

22.

WHAT ONE GIVES
ONE
RECEIVES.

WHEN THE HIGHEST SINCERITY IS REACHED
STRIPPED OF ALL EGO,
THE TAO
RESPONDS
AND
REVEALS ITS BEAUTY
IN
THE SIMPLE
AND
THE
MOST
ORDINARY.

23.

PARADOXICAL ARE THE WORDS OF GREAT
TRUTH.
NOTHING LASTS FOREVER.

GENTLE AND HOLY IS THE TRUE NATURE OF
THE TAO.

SHE SPEAKS TOO LOUDLY TO BE HEARD.
YET STILL, SHE WHISPERS AND IS HEARD.
TO BE ONE WITH HER IS TO FIND ONE'S INNER
TRUTH.
IN HER, ONE'S WEAKNESSES BECOME
STRENGTH.

THROUGH HER, WITHOUT EVEN SEARCHING,
ONE FINDS THEIR INNER STRENGTH.

THROUGH HER, WITHOUT EVEN SEARCHING,
ONE FINDS THEIR INNER TRUE NATURE.
CONNECTED TO HER UNIVERSAL TRUTH,
ONE DOES BY NOT DOING.
ONE THINKS BY NOT THINKING.

THE GREATEST TEACHER HAS NOTHING TO
SAY.
HE WHO ASKS ONLY TO SERVE IS GREATLY
FOLLOWED.

THE MASTER WORRIES NOT AND SIMPLY GOES
ABOUT HER WORK.
BY ONE STAYING, ONE DISCOVERS THE ENTIRE
WORLD
AS IT COMES TO CALL AT THEIR FEET.

(JUST GO WITH THE FLOW AND TRY NOT TO
OVERTHINK IT.)

24.

EPHEMERALLY,
AS THE PRIDEFUL, SELF RIGHTEOUS
AND POWERFUL FALL,

HER PATIENT, ETERNAL, AND RELENTLESS
NATURE
WEARS DOWN ALL,

SO THAT THE HUMBLE
MAY SOMEDAY
INHERIT THE EARTH.

25.

THE TAO,
IMMUTABLE PRESENCE,
THE NAMELESS GREAT ALL
ETERNALLY CALM,
FROM HER HEART
SHE REACHES OUTWARD
AND RETURNS UNTO HERSELF.

ALL FOLLOW HER
ONLY TO FIND HER ROOT
AND
ETERNAL LOVE
DWELLING PEACEFULLY WITHIN.

26.

AT ONE'S CENTER
IS THE BEAT OF THE HEART.
WHY LEAVE THE LOVE AND CARE OF SUCH A
HOME?

EVEN A ROLLING STONE MUST REST.

THOUGH A SAGE MUST TRAVEL FAR FROM
HOME
AT THE DAY'S JOURNEY'S END,
DESPITE THE VIEW AND BEAUTY OF THE
SUNSET
THE MASTER DOES NOT DEPART HASTILY
FROM
THE WINNEBAGO.

27.

ON ONE'S ETERNAL JOURNEY
UPON THE SUBTLE PATH
MORE THAN JUST HER BROTHER'S KEEPER,
SELFLESS, IMPARTIAL, CAREFUL MOTHER TO
ALL,
THE EMBODIMENT OF LIGHT,
INTUITIVELY,
THE SAGE GUIDES BY HER EXAMPLE
AND AVAILS HERSELF IMPARTIALLY
AND UNCONDITIONALLY TO ALL.

28.

TO BE STRONG,
BE GENTLE.

TO BE WISE,
BE KIND.

UNDERSTAND
WHAT YOU ARE.
KNOW
WHAT YOU ARE NOT.

ACCEPT WHAT IS.

THERE IS CENTERED IN ONE
THE PROVIDER TO ALL.

WITHIN THE JOY OF A CHILD,
PEACEFULLY AND SUBTLY
IT DWELLS.

29.

THE WONDROUS BEAUTY
OF
NATURAL PERFECTION
MAKES THE CLOCK
STAND STILL,
AS
ONE SEES THAT
THE HANDS
AND SANDS
THAT CONTROL TIME
ARE ANCHORED IN
THE RIVER OF TIMELESSNESS
AND
UPON
THE CENTER
WITHIN.

30.

VIOLENCE BEGETS VIOLENCE.
THE TAO BEGETS PEACE.
THESE TWO FORCES THE MASTER
UNDERSTANDS.

THE MASTER CANNOT CONTROL THE
UNIVERSE.
HE CAN ONLY CONTROL HIMSELF.

AND SO, THE MASTER
DIRECTS THE FLOW OF TAO,
AS HE PATIENTLY SETS ABOUT ITS WORK.

AS ONE MASTERS AND ACCEPTS THEMSELF,
SO TOO DOES THE WORLD ACCEPT
THE MASTER.

31.

THE MASTER KNOWS
THAT
THERE IS NOTHING OF HIGHER VALUE
THAN
PEACE.
SO, HE BOWS HIS HEAD IN DETEST
AS WAR ARRIVES.

FOR THE MASTER KNOWS
THAT
THISTLES GROW
WHERE CROPS ONCE THRIVED
AND THE WAGONS OF WAR WILL NOW TREAD.

THE MASTER UNDERSTANDS
NO GOOD WILL COME FROM WAR.
AS IT IS THE GAME OF FOOLS.
SO, THE MASTER ARMS FOR WAR
AND PRAYS THAT MERCY
AND FORGIVENESS FOLLOW
AND FOR PEACE
TO
SOMEDAY RULE OVER
THIS UNLEASHING OF HELL
THAT IS ABOUT TO OCCUR.

32.

UNIVERSAL SUBTLE ESSENCE,
MOTHER OF STARS,
THE RAIN
AND
THE SEASONS,
ETERNAL IS SHE.
YET TRANSITORY ARE ALL HER FORMS.
THOUGH RUGGED, PLAIN AND ORDINARY
MAY BE HER BEAUTY,
INFERIOR IS SHE TO NONE.

33.

TO EMBRACE DEATH AND NOT FEAR IT
IS CALLED "TO DIE WITHOUT DYING".

THE COWARD HAS TWO FACES
YET LIVES ONLY ONCE.

BUT THE HERO WITH A THOUSAND FACES
IS BORN ETERNAL.

34.

NOTHING OF SUBSTANCE IS FINAL.
WHAT IS REAL IN A REFLECTION?

THAT WHICH IS BEYOND REACH
REMAINS WITHIN IT.

ONE WHO LIVES THE TRUTH
NEEDS NOT HAVE AWARENESS OF IT.

THAT WHICH IS UNKNOWABLE
BY THE MIND
MAY READLY BE UNDERSTOOD
BY THE HEART.

35.

FIND PEACE AND PEACE WILL FIND YOU.
FEAR DEATH AND DEATH WILL FIND YOU.
FIND LOVE AND FEAR HAS NO PLACE.

36.

"THE SUBTLE TRUTH"

ONLY BY DISCARDING ALL
CAN ONE EMBRACE THEIR OWN TRUE
NATURE.
ONLY BY DISSOLVING THOUGHT
CAN ONE FULLY BE AWARE.

ONLY THE WEAKER CAN BECOME STRONGER.
ONLY BY CENTERING ONESELF IN PEACE,
CAN ONE GIVE THEMSELF OVER TO PAIN.

ONLY BY FORGIVENESS CAN ONE FULLY BE
RESTORED.
ONLY BY GIVING WHAT ONE HAS TO GIVE
CAN ONE RECEIVE ALL THAT ONE NEEDS.

ONLY BY THE SIMPLE UNDERSTANDING OF
THIS
CAN ONE KNOW "THE SUBTLE TRUTH".

37.

LOFTY ARE GOALS
BUT HARD WORK
IS SIMPLE.

BOTH TRAVEL
ON THE SAME ROAD
AS EACH

BECOMES
THE OTHER'S COMPANION.

38.

THE ELUSIVE TAO
AND THE TRUE HIDDEN SELF,
SHARE
SILENCE
AS THEIR SOUND.

NEITHER THE SELF NOR THE TAO
CAN BE EVER
TRULY LOST,
AS BOTH
ARE CAPABLE
OF FOREVER
BEING FOUND.

39.

NATURAL KINDNESS
MAKES BENEVOLENCE AND ETIQUETTE
UNNECESSARY.

AND SO, THE MASTER IS NATURALLY KIND.

NATURALLY HUMBLE AND UNPOLISHED,
HER BEAUTY
IS AS NATURAL
AS THE MOUNTAINS
AND
AS SOFT AND GENTLE AS A WINDING STREAM.

BY ENGENDERING
THE COMPASSIONATE SUBTLE ESSENCE OF
THE UNIVERSE,
SHE ATTAINS WISDOM,
AND KNOWS THEREBY NATURALLY
WHAT TO ACCEPT AND REJECT.

BY MAINTAINING BALANCE
AND BEING CENTERED WITHIN,
ALL IS HARMONIOUS
WHEREVER SHE GOES.

40.

"TAO"

UNFAILING,
VAST AND PROFOUND PRIMAL FEMALE,
THE MYSTERIOUS ORIGIN,
SEEN AND UNSEEN,
MYSTERIOUS INTERCOURSE
OF
YIN AND YANG,
MORE BEAUTIFUL THAT ANY WORDS CAN
TELL,

THE UNIVERSAL ETERNAL MOTHER,
IN ALL SOFTNESS,
YOU ARE SACRED.

FROM YOUR DIVINE SUBTLE ESSENCE
AND INDISCRIMINATE LOVE,
ALL THINGS ARE CREATED AND BROUGHT
FORTH
FROM YOUR SUBTLE REALM.

YOUR SUBTLE PATH AND I ARE ONE.

41.

WITHIN TAO
LIES THE TRUTH.
WITHIN THE TRUTH
LIES PARADOX.
WITHIN THE PARADOX
THERE IS TRUTH.

THE WISE EMBODY IT.
MADMEN AND FOOLS
LAUGH AT IT.

WHETHER ONE IS A WISE MAN,
A MADMAN
OR A FOOL,
THE TRUTH CARES NOT
WHO BELIEVES IT.

42.

THE "GREAT TRUTH"

IS THAT
WHAT ONE DOES OUTWARDLY TO OTHERS
ONE DOES INWARDLY TO ONESELF.
WHEN ONE CENTERS ONESELF AT HOME
WITHIN,
THEY CAN NEVER BE LOST IN THE UNIVERSE,
AS ALL ROADS RETURN THEM TO ONE'S
HOME.

43.

THE FULLNESS OF STONE
THE EMPTINESS OF SPACE,
BOTH ARE ILLUSION.

WHAT ONE SEES
AND WHAT ONE KNOWS
MATTER NOT
SHOULD THEY NOT LIVE BY THE TRUTH.

IF ONE DOES NOT KNOW FIRST TO LOVE
AND TO UNDERSTAND NEXT
THEY WILL CONTINUE TO LIVE AND DIE
IN A VIOLENT AND UNFORGIVING
IGNORANCE.

44.

'WHOLE VISION"

IS NO VISION
OF ANY THING IN PARTICULAR.
WEALTH, POVERTY, AFFECTION, LONELINESS,
SUCCESS, FAILURE,
THE MASTER'S HEART
NESTLED IN THE TAO
ACCEPTS THE IRRELEVANCE OF
EVERYTHING THAT BEFALLS IT.

FOR ONE WHO LIVES BY THEIR HEART'S
INTUITION,
THEIR COMPASS IS NEVER WITHOUT PROPER
DIRECTION.

45.

DOUBT IS EASY
AND TRUST DIFFICULT,
UNTIL ONE PROVES ONESELF TRUE.
IN TIME, TRUST BECOMES RELIANCE.

WHEN ONE TRUSTS AND RELIES
ON ONE WHO IS TRUE,
THEN, IN TRUTH, THERE IS NO RISK.

RELIANCE AND TRUST
THEN COME EASILY.
IT IS IN DOUBT THEN
THAT LIFE BECOMES DIFFICULT.

46.

FEAR
THE "SHIELD OF COWARDS",
IS THE "GREATEST AND MOST CRUEL OF ALL
ILLUSIONS".
THE MASTER TRUSTS IN THE TAO
AND SEES THROUGH FEAR,
AND SO THE MASTER IS SAFE.

WHEN THE TAO IS TRUSTED
FEAR DISAPPEARS.
WHEN FEAR DISAPPEARS, LOVE IS PRESENT.

WHEN LOVE IS PRESENT, NONE CAN BE
CALLED ENEMY.
WHEN THERE IS NO ENEMY, ALL IS SERENE.
WHEN SERENITY IS PRESENT, SO TOO IS PEACE.

COWARDS LIVE BY THEIR EGOS AND DIE IN A
STATE OF ISOLATION AND FEAR.

HEROES LIVE PEACEFULLY, COURAGEOUSLY,
SELFLESSLY AND WITH COMPASSION,
IN ONE WITH ALL.
THEY DIE IN A STATE OF LOVE
AND
IN THE COMPANY
OF THE DIVINE.

47.

THOSE WITHOUT HEARING
CAN HEAR THE BEATING OF THEIR OWN
HEARTS.
THOSE WITHOUT ARMS OR LEGS
MAY TOUCH THE HEARTS OF OTHERS.
EVEN THE BLIND WHO ARE WITHOUT SIGHT
CAN READ THE HUMAN HEART.
IT IS THE HEART THAT CONNECTS ALL TO
ONE
AND ONE TO ALL.

48.

MASTERY IN LIFE
IS ATTAINED
BY NOTHING MORE
THAN BY SIMPLY BEING IN THE MOMENT
AND BY ALLOWING THE TAO
TO TAKE ITS COURSE.

49.

WHEN THE MIND IS EMPTY OF THOUGHT
IT IS CAPABLE OF GOVERNING ALL.
ONE WITH TAO
THE MASTER TREATS ALL AS THEIR CHILDREN
EQUALLY WELL.
BY FULFILLING THEIR NEEDS,
ALL ARE AT PEACE.

50.

AS THE LIVING MOMENT INEVITABLY FADES,
AS ONE SURRENDERS TO DEATH, AND
ALLOWS IT, LIKE SLEEP TO OVERTAKE THEM,
WITH THE LAST BREATH
THE MASTER ALLOWS IT TO CARRY HIM ANON,
BACK INTO THE SUBTLE REALM
FROM WHENCE ALL THINGS COME
AND TO WHICH ALL THINGS RETURN
TO BE REBORN.

51.

TAO
UNIVERSAL CREATOR
AND
INTENDENT OF EVERYTHING.

NOURISHING ALL WITH LOVE
IN HER PEACE
THE MASTER
DOES ABIDE.

52.

TO "ABIDE IN THE TAO",

DESPITE ONE'S INFIRMITY,
IS TO "PRACTICE ETERNITY".

TO FOLLOW ONE'S INTERNAL FLAME
THE "I" AND "THOU",
ONE IN THE SAME.

ONE NEEDS NOT TO SEE
TO KNOW CLARITY
OR TO LOVE EXCLUSIVELY
TO KNOW CHARITY.

ONE MUST KNOW WHEN TO YIELD
AND WHEN TO FIGHT
AND REMEMBER THAT
AN OPEN MIND KEEPS THEIR HEART LIGHT.

OR THAT A MOTHER'S LOVE,
IMPARTIAL AND
FREE OF DESIRE,
LASTS IN US FOREVER,
AND THROUGH HER ETERNAL FIRE,
HER LIFE
AND LIGHT,
DO WE
TRANSCEND DEATH.

53.

MISERLY MATERIALISM,
THEFT, WAR, MISERY
AND PUSILLANIMITY
TRULY ARE NOT
ANY SUCH WAY
FOR ONE TO
HUMBLY
CENTER
ONESELF
IN THE
TAO.

54.

THE POEM OF THE INTEGRAL TAO

ONE OF INTEGRAL VIRTUE IS ONE WHO
KNOWS
TO FOLLOW ONLY THE SUBTLE LAW, THE TAO
ALONE.
ELUSIVE, EVASIVE, SHADOWY ENIGMA,
UNIVERSAL MYSTERY, SUBTLE-ENERGY,
SHE DISCLOSES HER SECRETS.
REALITY'S MYSTERIOUS ESSENCE
WITH UNFAILING CERTAINTY
ONE MAY KNOW HER
SUBTLE REALITY
AND, LIKE HER,
REJOIN
BY
RETURNING
AND GENTLY WORKING
TIRELESSLY TO BRING FORTH
THE MANIFEST FROM THE UNMANIFEST.
SOFTEST OF SOFT, SHE, LIKE WATER
PENETRATES BOTH SPACE AND SPACELESS
ALIKE
TO COMPLETE BOTH THE POSSIBLE AND
IMPOSSIBLE.
WITHOUT HER, NOTHING IS DONE OR LEFT
UNDONE.

TO KNOW THE BENEFIT OF SILENCE AND
NON-ACTION,
IS TO UNDERSTAND ALL, THOUGH UNDER
HEAVEN, FEW CAN.

55.

THE TAO'S LOVING FERTILITY
NOURISHES ALL THAT TAKE ROOT
AND
FIND STABILITY IN HER SOIL.

SONGS AND SONGSTRESS
OF THE INFINITE UNIVERSES
THANK YOU.
YOUR LIGHT SINGS.
YOUR STARS
ARE YOUR NOTES
STRUNG TOGETHER
IN AN ETERNAL TUNE.

YOUR SONG IS ENDLESS.
IT SINGS TO US AT BIRTH
AND
WHEN OUR BODY DIES.

THOUGH ALL PATHS
LEAD FROM YOU AND TO YOU,
YOU REMAIN HERE AT HOME
IN MY BEATING HEART.

56.

BEHOLD THE NEWBORN,
SUPPLE EMBODIMENT OF ALL LIFE,
HARMONIOUS, FRESH, VITAL.
TO YOU,
ALL IS ONE.

A LIVING TAI CHI,
INNOCENT OF DICHOTOMY.
YOUR ANCIENT SPIRIT INTACT,
AGAIN, BORN ANEW,
WE CELEBRATE AND WELCOME YOU.

57.

THERE IS WISDOM
IN SILENCE.
SO, BE SILENT.
THERE IS LOVE IN LISTENING
SO, LISTEN.
THERE IS COMPASSION IN PATIENCE
SO, BE PATIENT.

LET THE DUSTS THAT SURROUND YOU
SETTLE.
LET YOUR VISION BECOME CRYSTAL CLEAR.
LET THE TAO UNTIE THE KNOTS THAT BIND
YOU.
ALLOW THEM TO LOOSEN
AND THEN SIMPLY LISTEN AND JUST BE.

FIND IN YOUR SILENCE: PEACE.
IN YOUR LISTENING: LOVE
IN YOUR COMPASSION: UNDERSTANDING,
IN GIVING: HAPPINESS
IN TIME: ETERNITY
IN THE TAO: ALL.

58.

A GREAT LEADER TRUSTS AND FOLLOWS THE
TAO.
HE LETS IT GOVERN ALL.

FLEXIBLE AS WATER,
LITTLE DOES HE CARVE IN STONE.

HE PROHIBITS LITTLE
AND ALLOWS HIS PEOPLE MUCH.

IN THEIR SELF RELIANCE, ALL ARE SECURE.

THE MASTER WHO GOVERNS BEST IS ONE
WHO LIVES SIMPLY,
ACTS PATIENTLY
AND ASKS LITTLE OF THE COMMON WEAL.

59.

IN GOVERNANCE
IT IS TOLERANCE THAT BEARS FRUIT
AND REPRESSION THAT BREEDS CONTEMPT.

WHEN GOVERNMENT STRIVES TO
ACCOMPLISH,
IT ACHIEVES THE OPPOSITE.

THE COURSE OF HONOR IS NOT EASILY
EARNED.
THE ONE WHO GOVERNS BEST LEADS BY
EXAMPLE.

BECAUSE THE MASTER LOVES PEACE
HE FOLLOWS THE INTEGRAL WAY.

BECAUSE HE LOVES LIFE
HE ALLOWS THE TAO TO FLOURISH.

THE MASTER GOVERNS SELFLESSLY
AND SERVES ALL BY NON-DOING.

HE TRUSTS THAT HIS PEOPLE KNOW
WHAT IS BEST FOR THEMSELVES.
AND FOR THEIR NEEDS,
THE TAO PROVIDES.

BECAUSE HIS SWORD REMAINS SHEATHED
HIS GOVERNANCE IS NOT POINTLESS BUT
PEACEFUL.

THE GREAT MASTER EXUDES RADIANCE.
BECAUSE OF HIS GREATNESS, THE PEOPLE ARE
ALWAYS GLAD TO SEE HIM.

60.

THE MASTER GOVERNS ALL WITH
MODERATION

FREE FROM HER OWN IDEAS, SHE USES ALL
THAT COMES HER WAY.

TOLERANT AND INSIGHTFUL,
FLEXIBLE BUT FIRM,
WITHOUT THOUGHT OF THE POSSIBLE,
NOTHING BECOMES IMPOSSIBLE,
AS SHE ALLOWS THE TAO TO GOVERN
AND OVERCOMES ALL WITH A MOTHER'S
NATURAL LOVE.

61.

GOVERNANCE

IS LIKE GRILLING A TINY FISH.

IF POKED AND OVERTENDED
THE FISH CRUMBLES FROM OVERATTENTION.
AS THE FISH IS PRODDED,
IT BECOMES UNCENTERED.
AND IT WILL FALL THROUGH THE CRACKS
AND DISAPPEARS
INTO THE FLAMES.

62.

BOTH GREAT NATIONS AND GREAT MEN
KNOW HUMILITY.
THEY KNOW THAT
MISTAKES ARE BEST EARLY FIXED.
CORRECTIONS OBLIGED,
TO BE ENEMY TO NONE.
AND SO,
THE GREAT NATION
AGAINST OR BETWIXT
BECOMES ONE.

63.

TAO
ALPHA AND OMEGA,
AT THE CENTER OF ALL,
THE WISE SEEK ITS TREASURE,
THE BAD, ITS REFUGE.

ALL RECEIVE ITS FORGIVENESS.
BECAUSE OF THIS SHE IS

BELOVED BY ALL WHO KNOW HER.

64.

WHEN STEPS SMALL BECOME
ONE'S DIFFICULTIES
ARE OVERCOME
AND THE GREAT ACT
DONE.
ONE'S PROBLEMS REMAIN SMALL
WHEN DEALT WITH EARLY ALL.

AND BY RELEASING HOLD
OF ONE'S OWN COMFORT
EVEN PROBLEMS OLD
DISAPPEAR.

65.

THE NEW SPROUT GROWS FAST
ONCE ARE ITS ROOTS FIRM AND CALM.

IT MAY BE NOURISHED AND DIRECTED EARLY.
UNHURRIED,
WHEN MATURE AND FULLY GROWN
IT RELEASES ITS FRUIT
AND IS REBORN
TO NOURISH ALL.

66.

THE MASTER
KNOWS NOTHING

OTHER THAN THAT, HE KNOWS NOT.
THUS, THE MASTER MAY COME TO
UNDERSTAND ALL.

FINDING PEACEFUL CONTENTMENT
IN THE SIMPLE AND ORDINARY,
THE MASTER RETURNS
TO HER OWN TRUE NATURE.

67.

THE POWER OF THE SEA LIES IN ITS LOWNESS.
BECAUSE IT IS LOW,
LIKE THE STREAMS AND RIVERS TO HER
DEPTHS
ALL ARE DRAWN TO IT.

THE SAME IS TRUE
WITH GREAT COUNTRIES AND GREAT
LEADERS.

TO BE A GREAT TEACHER
ONE MUST FIRST BE A GREAT STUDENT.

TO BE A GREAT LEADER,
ONE MUST LEARN TO BE A GOOD FOLLOWER.
TEACHER, STUDENT, LEADER FOLLOWER,
EVENTUALLY ONE BECOMES THE OTHER.

68.

THE "THREE GREAT TREASURES":
SIMPLICITY, PATIENCE AND LASTLY,
COMPASSION.

TO RETURN TO ONE'S TAO SOURCE,
THERE IS NO TREASURE GREATER THAN
COMPASSION.
FOR ONESELF,
ALL THE OTHERS ARE MERE DETAILS.

69.

THE GREATEST COMPETITORS
TEST THEMSELVES AGAINST THE BEST
COMPETITION.
BUT EACH KNOWS
IT IS WITH THEMSELF ALONE THAT HE OR
SHE TRULY COMPETES.

HE WHO SERVES THE BEST, SERVES THE MANY.

WHEN ONE'S LIFE'S WORK
BECOMES LIKE A CHILD'S PLAY
THEY MAY BE CALLED "MASTER",
FOR THE MASTER AND THE TAO ARE ONE.

70.

ONE WHO LOSES THEIR THREE GREAT
TREASURES
FINDS SOON
THAT VICTORY RETREATS
AND ABUNDANCE SLIPS FROM THEIR GRASP.

BY RETAINING SIMPLICITY, PATIENCE, AND
COMPASSION,
ONE'S INWARD THREE TREASURES,
AND BY KNOWING WHEN AND HOW TO GIVE
AND WHEN TO YIELD
ONE BECOMES BOTH VICTORIOUS AND
ABUNDANT.

71.

OLDER THAN TIME,
THE TAO'S SIMPLE TEACHINGS
ARE UNIVERSAL,
EASILY UNDERSTOOD
AND FOLLOWED.

TO OVERTHINK THEM
IS TO FAIL.

ONE NOT NEED TO GO OUTSIDE
OF ONE'S OWN HEART
TO FOLLOW ITS PATH
OR KNOW ITS TRUTH.

72.

ONE'S COMFORT IS A SICKNESS,
ONE'S IGNORANCE, A DISEASE.

THE MASTER UNDERSTANDS
THAT HE DOES NOT KNOW,
AND PIERCES IGNORANCE
SO THAT
HE MAY HEAL HIMSELF
OF ALL KNOWING AND NOT KNOWING.

73.

LIFE WITHOUT AWE
LEAVES ONLY RELIGION.
WHEN ONE TRUSTS ONESELF
THEY NEED NOT TRUST IN AUTHORITY.

A TEACHER TEACHES
WHAT OTHERS NEED TO LEARN.

BUT THE MASTER TEACHES NOTHING
AND
SIMPLY SETS FORTH AN EXAMPLE
SO THAT NOTHING NEEDS TO BE TAUGHT.
THIS IS "TEACHING WITHOUT TEACHING".

74.

IN SILENT EASE SHE SPEAKS.
SHE COMES WITHOUT A CALL.

HER ANSWER COMES TO EVERY QUESTION.
WITHIN HER HEAVENLY NET
THE TAO HOLDS
AND OVERCOMES ALL.

75.

WHEN THE PEOPLE FORGET THE TAO,
THEY RELY ON RELIGIONS AND THEIR DOGMA
AND ON GOVERNMENT AND ITS LAWS.
BOTH ARE DOOMED TO FAIL.
FOR GOVERNMENT TO TAX THE POOR
AND
INTRUDE ON THE PEACE OF ALL,
BENEFITS NONE.

HE WHO GOVERNS BEST
TRUSTS THE PEOPLE MOST
AND
TAXES AND INTRUDES IN THEIR LIVES
THE LEAST.

76.

THE HARD AND UNYIELDING FAIL.

READY FOR THE AXE,
QUICKLY THE TREE FALLS
THAT DOES NOT BEND.

SOFT AND SUPPLE ARE THE
"DISCIPLES OF LIFE".

77.

THE BOW OF THE TAO
BALANCED AND FLEXED
RELAXED AND SUPPLE,
IT TAKES FROM THE GREATER
AND GIVER TO THE LESSER.

NO FORCE IS HER EQUAL,
AS HER HUMBLE NATURE IS
TO PROVIDE FOR THE NEEDS OF ALL
IN ABUNDANCE.

78.

WATER IS PATIENT,
BOTH GENTLE AND STRONG,
IT YIELDS, YET IT CAN BE RELENTLESS.

TRUTH IS PARADOXICAL.

THE SERENE MASTER
IS MOST LIKE WATER.

BECAUSE HE IS WATER,
THERE IS NOTHING HE CANNOT OVERCOME.

79.

ONCE ONE UNDERSTANDS ETERNITY,
PATIENCE BECOMES EASY.

ONCE SIMPLICITY IS UNDERSTOOD,
THEN LIFE BECOMES EASY AND WITHOUT
STRIVING.

WHEN ONE UNDERSTANDS COMPASSION,
THERE IS ALWAYS ROOM
FOR GRATITUDE AND ABUNDANCE.

TO THE MASTER,
FAILURE AND SUCCESS
MEAN NOTHING.

THE MASTER DOES NOT FRET.
HE SIMPLY ACCEPTS WHAT IS.

THE MASTER RECTIFIES SELFLESSLY.
KNOWING HIMSELF FALLIBLE.

NO MATTER WHERE HE DWELLS
BLAME HAS NO PLACE.

80.

SIMPLE LABOR
MAKES THE HANDS
AND HEART
CONTENT.

THE WELL-GOVERNED
STAY PEACEFULLY
AT HOME,
FOR THEY KNOW
THAT THE GRASS IS GREENEST
WHEREVER THEIR FAMILY
AND
LOVED ONES
DWELL.

81.

WORDS THAT ARE TRUE
ARE NOT ELEQUENT.
THOSE THAT ARE ELOQUENT
NOT TRUE.
THE WISE KNOW THERE IS NOTHING
NEED THEY PROVE.
WITHOUT FORCE THE TAO NOURISHES.
WITHOUT DOMINATION
THE MASTER LEADS.
POSSESSING NOTHING
BUT GRATITUDE,
GREAT IS THE MASTER'S WEALTH.

82.

THE SONG OF THE GREAT TAI CHI

THE SUBTLE ESSENCE OF THE UNIVERSE IS
ETERNAL.
IT IS LIFE'S UNFAILING FOUNTAIN,
WHICH FLOWS FOREVER IN A VAST AND
PROFOUND VALLEY VERNAL
FROM THE VAST AND TIMELESS MOUNTAIN.
SHE IS CALLED PRIMAL FEMALE,
THE "MYSTERIOUS ORIGIN" IS HER TALE.
THE UNIVERSE'S OPENING AND CLOSING
OF THE GATE OF ORIGIN WITHOUT FAIL,
SHE PERFORMS THE MYSTICAL INTERCOURSE
OF THE UNIVERSE,
THE MAGICAL DANCE THAT BRINGS FORTH
ALL THINGS
FROM THE UNSEEN REALM INTO THE
MANIFEST DIVERSE.
WHEN ONE HEARS THE WIND, IT IS SHE THAT
SINGS.
THE MYSTICAL INTERCOURSE OF YIN AND
YANG
IS THE ROOT OF UNIVERSAL LIFE,
THE SUBTLE GENTLE MOVEMENT OF THE
INTERPLAY OF THIS NEVER-CEASING PLAN, TAI
CHI CREATES BOTH PEACE AND STRIFE.
ITS CREATIVITY AND USEFULNESS ARE
BOUNDLESS

HERS IS LIFE WITHOUT END
AND WHEN OUR LIVES ARE OVER, SOUNDLESS
ONWARD OUR SOULS SHE WILL SEND.

FIN

ABOUT THE AUTHOR

N. Michael Murburg, Jr., "Mike", is a graduate of Princeton University, (B.A., 1977) where he received the honor of being named class poet in 2017. While at Princeton he took studies in the Departments of History, Religion and Classics. Mike is also an honors graduate of the Florida State University College of Law and a practicing attorney. Mike began writing poetry at age 11 and has not ceased. Although his recitations have reached millions, this work written between 2015 and 2024 is his first written published work, of poetry.

www.ingramcontent.com/pod-product-compliance
Lightning Source LLC
Chambersburg PA
CBHW020740160726
47993CB00006B/2541